Little Sylvie
An Unforgettable Adoption Story

To contact the author,
TheSylvieGStory@gmail.com

ISBN-13: 978-1544775203
ISBN-10: 1544775202

Little Sylvie
An Unforgettable Adoption Story

Chapter 1 7
Chapter 2 11
Chapter 3 13
Chapter 4 19
Chapter 5 21
Chapter 6 23
Chapter 7 27
Chapter 8 33
Chapter 9 37
Chapter 10 41
Chapter 11 47
Chapter 12 49
Chapter 13 53
Chapter 14 55
Chapter 15 57
Chapter 16 59
Chapter 17 63
Chapter 18 65
Chapter 19 71
Chapter 20 75
Chapter 21 79
Chapter 22 81
Chapter 23 85

Dedicated to My Parents

To my dear Dad… You were there for me, day in and day out. Then when necessary, I was there for you, every day. I am not sure if you actually knew I was there sometimes. But I am willing to bet that you knew how much I cared for and appreciated you. You "saved the day" all my life, always solving problems, and rescuing me from the world. You saved my life, literally and figuratively. I only wish I could have saved yours.

And to my Mom… You do everything for everyone, literally. You taught me when I was young that I "*can do anything if I put my mind to it.*" Well, I used that advice over and over again, in my personal, school, and business life, beating the odds more than once. It was your work ethic, honesty, and strong mind that have inspired me all these years. Thanks Mom…

Chapter 1

It all started when Ann and Joseph wanted a second child. They already adopted a girl through an agency in Brooklyn, but the adoption process this time seemed to be more difficult. They completed mountains of paperwork, had plenty of home visits, had to prove they would be worthy of a second child while continuing to allow the adoption agency to monitor the first adoption. The first baby was just 8 months old when she was adopted. The application process took years. It was incredibly demanding of the couple's time and energy, but this is what they wanted more than anything. They wanted a family to raise and cherish and they wanted their family to grow for years to come.

Joseph was a tradesman. He had steady work, but it was not a 6 figure salary. It was respectable and he enjoyed his work. Joseph took pride in his work and was a reliable employee. The agency respected that and gave him a passing grade on career. His loving wife Ann worked in retail. That was not an easy career as far as schedule, physical efforts, or salary. Still, the agency approved it. They respected this young couple's desire to provide a great home for their children.

Joseph and Ann had plenty of relatives who were supportive, loving, and willing to help if necessary. Each holiday included a family gathering at someone's home. It almost always included plenty of great food, a game after dinner, and lots of laughter. This was the type of family the agency wanted to place children in. The workers that directly communicated with Joseph and Ann really worked at moving the applications along, but the system required a long, difficult application process.

A recent communication with the couple stated that there were no male babies in NYC to adopt. They could however drive up to Canada to meet a baby boy. The discussions between Joseph and Ann were long and meaningful. They could easily drive up to Canada, but would it be worth their time and energy? What if the baby up there didn't immediately become attached? What if they had problems crossing the border in either direction? They would both have to take time off from work for the trip. They only hoped it would all work out.

Joseph and Ann wanted a boy because they already had a baby girl, Marie. She was thriving and they wanted to give her a sibling. Their daughter was already highly intelligent, speaking nearly non-stop, and very happy at three years old.

Chapter 2

Joseph yelling from the kitchen, "*Did you remember to pack snacks for the ride? And what about drinks?*" Ann, knowing Joseph well responded from the bedroom with, "*yes, your favorite cookies and cans of soda are in the cooler. And there are rest stops along the way.*" Joseph goes back out to the porch and sees the cooler along with some other bags to be packed into the Plymouth. He grabbed the luggage first for the trunk and then he placed the cooler on the floor in passenger side so it would be easy for Ann to reach. Ann popped her head out the door, "*Did you fit all the bags in the trunk? Do we have enough room for your parents and their bags? What about Marie's bag of books and toys?*" Joseph noticed it next to the driver's side on the ground and sighed. Another bag into the car and it looked like his parents and the baby would hardly fit after all the bags. So the car was packed and they were off to pick up Joseph's parents for the long drive to Canada.

Everyone fit in the car comfortably and it was a smooth ride up to Canada. At the border they only asked what their business would be and if they had anything to declare. A quick check in the car and they were on their way to the orphanage. Many of the road signs in Montreal were in French and the drivers seemed to go really fast. Grace blurting out, *"what's his rush?"* as a car cut them off by an exit. Grace, Joseph's mom was a true, kind, lady with a sweet sense of humor. Joseph's father, Joseph Senior, was a quiet, caring man who sat back and watched the interactions of everyone else.

Ann getting more nervous by the moment, *"Do you think they'll like us? They do not have to give us a baby even though we've been approved you know."* Joseph, also a bit nervous, but never showing it, gave Ann a reassuring smile. *"We'll be fine. We're almost there, just a few more minutes."* The four adults and young Marie sat quietly for the last few minutes of the trip.

Chapter 3

After several hours and a few quick stops along the way they arrived at the orphanage in Montreal Canada. They exited the car stiff from the long ride. Surprisingly, the first one to break the silence was Joseph senior. "*Do you want us to wait out here? We can sit on the bench over there.*" A nervous look is exchanged between Joseph and Ann. Not sure what to do, Ann responded, "*Don't be silly. You're the grandparents.*"

The walked into a musty smelling, dark, dingy waiting area. It had old chairs and the walls looked like they could use a good painting. They saw a few nuns passing the doorway in the back and then were approached by one middle aged nun who looked like she hadn't slept in a decade.

"*You must be Joseph and Ann. And who is this with you?*" Ann proudly held up Marie and said, "*this is the older sister. And these are Josephs parents. We hope it is ok that we brought everyone.*" The nun had no expression on her face, but her response was friendly and welcoming. "*Yes, it's good that we get to meet grandparents. That normally doesn't happen. Stay here and I will check on the baby."*

Ann and Joseph look around and each hoped for a smooth afternoon with the orphanage and new baby. The nun returned with a clipboard and a concerned look on her face. *"So sorry, the boy you came to meet is not here. He is actually in the hospital with health problems. We don't think he'll make it, but we do have a little girl who desperately needs a good home."*

Ann's eyes filled up and Joseph remained quiet as he put his arm around Ann. They looked at each other, knowing they really wanted a boy. This was a long application process and they were told there was a boy at this orphanage. That is why they took the long drive, to adopt a little boy.

They remained quiet for a long moment when the nun interrupted, *"Can I at least bring out the little girl for you to hold for a few minutes?"* Exhausted from the long drive and not wanting to appear they would not be good parents they agreed. The nun quickly disappeared and Grace with her compassion and sweet sense of humor said, *"You drove all the way here and you can always say you'll wait for a boy. I wonder if you can get a rain check.*" She did lighten the mood a bit before the nun brought out the other baby.

In dirty, torn clothes and drastically underweight Sylvie was handed to Ann. She was over one year old, but she was so small that the couple thought she was younger. Not speaking the same language, little Sylvie and Ann just stared at each other. Little Sylvie carefully studied Ann's face and reached for her as if to hug her. Joseph observed and knew that little girl was going home with them sometime soon. And little Marie quietly stared at Sylvie as she sat in Grace's lap across the room.

They sat in that room for an hour. Not much conversation, just observing this little baby who desperately needed a home. Ann did say a few things to the baby, "*I bet I can fatten you up. You'd have a big sister. Do you want to come home with us?* "

Joseph just reached for little Sylvie's hand and held it. Joseph's thoughts were that he wanted a boy, but he seemed to be falling for this little girl. And to watch his wife hold this baby and immediately bond, he knew Sylvie would complete their family. Ann and joseph exchanged a few loving looks without words.

They knew there would be time to talk when they left the orphanage.

The nun returned to the waiting room to see the bond already beginning between the family and the baby. She smiled as she said, "*I'm sorry, it's time for Sylvie's dinner.*" She hated to break it up, but had to bring the baby in the back for her dinner. With so many children, they had to stick to their schedule.

As the nun attempted to take little Sylvie she felt some resistance. Sylvie was holding Anne's sweater and would not let go. She did not want to leave the safety of Ann's arms. Little Sylvie started to cry as the nun took her away from Ann. Ann grew a pump in her throat as she watched little Sylvie disappear with the nun into the back. The nun then returned to the waiting room.

The nun commented, "*That went well. Would you be willing to come back tomorrow after sleeping on this decision? This baby really does need a home. She will not survive here much longer. We try to feed her, but she is still very underweight. We have so many children desperate for homes. We really do try our best.*"

Ann and Joseph agreed and thanked the nun for their time.

Ann and Joseph promised to return early the next day. The nun gave a few final words for them to sleep on, "*she really NEEDS you to take her home. I'm honestly not sure how long she will last here. I saw the same thing happen with the little boy.*" The boy was the same way, but his condition worsened. He came in shortly before Sylvie.

As the family exited the orphanage, Grace suggested they find a place to eat dinner and a hotel to get some rest before the next morning.

Chapter 4

A good dinner and some sleep is what the family needed. They found a hotel first, checked in, and asked where they could get dinner. Just up the street was a family restaurant and they had a few waiters who spoke English.

Everyone was hungry and the restaurant offered large enough portions to satisfy the hungriest people. Before discussing Sylvie they consumed their food, appreciated the décor, and were very happy with the service. They all knew Sylvie needed to become part of their family.

Before tea and coffee arrived at the table, Ann broke the silence. Her eyes started to fill up, "*Joseph, we NEED to make her ours. She will not survive in that awful place much longer.*" Joseph wasn't one for long conversations, his response was quick and to the point. "*I know.*" Ann added, "*She'll DIE in that place. We can't let that happen.*" Again Joseph agreed, took Ann's hand and said, "*Sylvie will be ours. Do you think we'll take her home tomorrow or is there more paperwork?*" Grace chimed in, "*I bet we'll have to come back another time. I can't imagine it would happen so fast.*" And then

Joseph Senior said, "*Grace, we really don't know the Canadian system. They seem pretty desperate to give her a home.*"

The group had their tea and coffee and continued to discuss their new family member, all hoping they'd get the formal approval from this orphanage. Grace adding with a smile, "*we'll need to go shopping for all new clothes for her. That outfit did nothing for her little figure.*" Ann smiled for the first time since yesterday. Her nerves were really shot and the exhaustion was setting in.

Chapter 5

After dinner and a good night's sleep the family made their way back to the orphanage. Feeling fresh and optimistic about the future the family walked into the dingy waiting room. They could immediately smell the dust in the air and other unpleasant odors. Ann and Joseph knew they were not adopting a boy as planned. They were going to add an underweight, malnourished little girl to their family. Little Sylvie needed a home and they knew they could give her that.

The nun looking fresh and ready for her day gave a cheerful, "*good morning everyone.*" A bit surprised at the nun's good mood Ann and Joseph smiled and responded appropriately. Surprisingly, Joseph was the first to speak, "*so what happens now?*" The nun, a little confused, "*did you make a decision already?*" With an enthusiastic tone, "*Let me get Sylvie for another visit.*" She quickly disappeared.

Ann just looked at Joseph in shock that he was so quick to get things rolling. Joseph responded to her expression with, "*what?*" Ann said, "*I think you shocked her, she didn't get her a chance to tell us what's next.*" Before another response could be exchanged, the nun appeared with Sylvie.

Big sister Marie was so well behaved through the whole trip. She looked at Sylvie and just said, "*sister.*" Everyone was a bit surprised. Marie did talk often, but was pretty quiet during this trip. She evidently heard and processed all the adult conversations over the past 24 hours. The nun, hands to her cheeks and an expression of adoration just said, "*I hope so little one.*" She knew the topic and end result of the discussions just by Marie's two words.

The nun asked Ann if she should get the papers for her and Joseph to sign. Sylvie once again looked very comfortable in Ann's arms. It already looked like a beautiful family photo, even with the dingy surroundings. Grace and Joseph senior remained pretty quiet most of the time observing Ann and little Sylvie. They looked very happy to be getting another granddaughter. Grace said, "*I think she really took to you Ann.*" Ann not taking her eyes off Sylvie, "*I'd say.*"

Chapter 6

Joseph took the papers from the nun and began to read. The nun quickly went into the back to attend to a few crying children. Joseph took a pen out of his pocket and began to go through the papers. *"Didn't we answer all these questions through our adoption agency?"* Ann answered, *"please just do it, we already jumped through hoops. This is the smallest stack of papers we've seen. It could be the last ones we'll have to sign."* There were several spaces for signatures and other information. He asked Ann for some answers and knew others without asking.

Within a few minutes, the papers completed and signed by Ann and Joseph, Grace said, *"well little Sylvie, looks like you'll be a Brooklynite soon enough."* Ann and Sylvie seemed inseparable at this point. The nun, beginning to show the stress of her day returned. Already wet marks on her clothes. One of the kids had thrown a bottle in a tantrum. The crying could be heard everywhere in the building. The loud cries made Ann and Joseph more eager to bring Sylvie home with them as soon as possible. The nun was right, Sylvie needed to be placed in a good home as soon as possible. The nun's first words upon entry into the waiting area, "*Good the papers are complete?*" A simultaneous "*yes*" from Ann and Joseph. "*Then I'll get things moving. Next we need to confirm everything, call the adoption agency one more time in Brooklyn, and call your references*". Ann and Joseph looked at each other for a long moment, hope in their eyes. They knew they were going home without Sylvie, but Ann asked the nun, "*so this means we can't take Sylvie today?*" The nun said, "*yes, I'm sorry. All of this work cannot be done in a day. Not all the calls and reference checks will be competed in a day.*" Joseph looked disappointed and asked, "*how much longer can we stay today?*" The nun gave a look of compassion saying, "*I can see Sylvie belongs with you, but we can only give you a few more minutes. We must continue on with our schedule.*" Soon to be big sister Marie, standing next to Sylvie, decided to give her a kiss on the arm. Everyone smiled quietly at the two little girls.

"*OK, so sorry, but time is up.*" The nun hurrying into the area to take Sylvie back to her bed. "*I must get her in for her nap and start cleaning.*" As she reached for Sylvie, a shrieking cry came from Sylvie's mouth. Grace laughed and said, *"well, we better buy some earplugs soon."* Ann, with eyes filling up handed Sylvie to the nun, knowing she'd be back for her soon.

The family quietly walked out of the orphanage into the bright sun. Squinting, Joseph suggested they stop for lunch before getting back on the road to Brooklyn. They had a filling meal and then a long ride back to Brooklyn, without their little Sylvie.

Chapter 7

Ann and Joseph went back to their regular lives and waited for the long adoption process to play out. Each week Ann called the adoption agency for updates and it did seem to be moving along, but not at the speed she wanted. One Saturday afternoon, Ann asked Joseph, "*What if something happens before we bring her home?*" A surprised look, from Joseph sitting at the kitchen table, responded with, "*don't be silly, what would happen?*" A scared look on Anne's face, "*you saw how skinny she was… and you heard the nun say she would not last much longer in the orphanage. What if…*" Joseph quickly cut her off, "*No, don't think like that. That little baby will hold on. I bet she knows she is coming home soon.*"

Ann placed her sandwich on the table and as soon as she sat down the phone rang. "*Oh, who could that be on a Saturday afternoon?*" Joseph stopped eating to answer the phone. "*Yes, this is he. Hello. Yes, she is here with me. That's good news! When can we come get her?*" The entire time Ann looked at Joseph in confusion, then with the final question she dropped her sandwich and jumped up to try to listen to the call with Joseph. Tears in her eyes, an excited, *"thank you."*

And finally, after 6 weeks, they were approved and allowed to pick up their daughter at any time. In the middle of July they took the trip back up to Canada to make their family complete. The car loaded up again with Joseph, Ann, little Marie, and Joseph's parents Grace and Joseph Sr. The ride was happier this time, all were looking forward to bringing Sylvie home. Grace turned to Marie and said, *"are you happy to be a big sister?"* And Marie enthusiastically shook her head as she continued to look out the window. Just about an hour away from the orphanage the anticipation could be felt.

This family was tired from the drive, but happy the long process of papers would come to an end. They knew it would be a long, interesting drive home the next day with a new family member. They could not wait to start watching Sylvie grow up with her big sister Marie.

The family arrived and walked into the dirty, foul-smelling orphanage. They could not wait to get their younger daughter out of that atmosphere. After waiting a moment, the nun came out front. She said, *"ah, the whole crew again. I'll go get Sylvie and one final paper for you to sign.*" And Grace let out, "*oh, my, more papers?*" Joseph Sr just looked at her as if she should not have said that out loud. Ann and Joseph stood close to each other, patiently waiting to see their younger daughter. "*I can't wait to give her some fresh air.*" Ann said, followed with, "*and a good meal.*"

As the nun approached with Sylvie, she dove into Ann's arms as if she knew where she belonged. Joseph let out a small laugh and kissed his new daughter on the head. The nun handed the final paper to be signed to Joseph with a smile on her face. "*Sylvie needs a good home. Thank you for taking her. Have a blessed and happy life little girl.*"

On that July day in 1967, all the formalities were done and the family walked out, happy, tired, and ready to begin the next chapter I their lives.

The ride home was interesting. There was a good amount of traffic at the border into the USA from Canada. Grace said as they sat and waited their turn, "*I wonder what they'll ask this time. Maybe the same questions as last time.*" Just a few cars away from the patrol officer Joseph opened his window. "*Good evening folks. Where are you headed?*" Joseph responded, "*Home.*" The patrol officer next asked, "*What is the purpose of your travel?*" Joseph responded with, "*vacation.*" And the final question from the border patrol officer was, "*Do you have anything to claim?*" Joseph said "*no.*" And from the back seat Grace said, "*the baby.*" By that time the officer moved away from the vehicle and everyone had a good laugh.

From that point on, the ride was smooth, everyone tired and quiet. They made it home late that night.

"*Good thing we set everything up before we left.*" Ann said in a hushed voice. Both little girls were sleeping as they pulled into their driveway. The lights were on downstairs so Ann knew her father was still awake. Suddenly, she felt exhilarated as she exited the car and lifted Sylvie. Joseph lifted Marie out as she slept. Both were gently placed in their room for a good night's sleep. Ann just watched both girls sleep a while as Joseph unpacked the car. Finally they met in the living room to unwind a bit before they went to bedroom. Satisfied, tired, and waiting for the rest of their lives to start. They lied in bed and Ann's final words to Joseph as they drifted to sleep that night, "*we did it.*

After all this time, we finally have both our girls here with us." Joseph half sleeping already said, "*yes, it was a good day.*" Ann's final words before they both drifted to sleep, "*I'll have to fatten her up a bit.*"

Chapter 8

Joseph was a morning person, up by dawn most days. It was just after 7am the next morning and Joseph was sitting on the front porch reading the newspaper. He had about an hour of quiet before he heard movement inside. He walked in to see his three favorite people in the kitchen. Ann was preparing breakfast for the girls and they were sitting quietly. Marie was watching everything Sylvie did in amazement. Joseph broke the silence with, "*Do you like your baby sister Marie?*" Marie looked up at Joseph, surprised to see him and smiled. "*Here you go Marie.*" Ann placed a plate with cut up French toast in front of her. Ann then sat next to Sylvie to feed her some hot cereal. She ate some then Ann gave her a bottle. At 14 months old, Sylvie was very underweight and Ann had a plan to bring her to a healthy weight.

After breakfast Ann decided to bring the girls on the porch. It was a nice summer day and Sylvie needed fresh air as much as she needed good food. A neighbor passed and waved on her way to the corner market. And on her way back from the corner market that neighbor stopped. "*Who is the baby?*" Ann, with a great sense of pride said, "*This is Sylvie, my younger daughter.*" The neighbor was surprised, not knowing the long process Joseph and Ann just endured to finally bring Sylvie home. "*Oh, that's great, congratulations. What a cute little one. I better get this milk in my fridge. I'm so happy for you.*" As the neighbor climbed down the stairs another neighbor came out. Their porch was adjacent to Ann and Joseph's porch. The neighbor, Elaine, asked "*Who is this little one?*" And Ann picked Sylvie up out of the playpen and showed her to Elaine. With excitement in her eyes, Ann said, "*This is Sylvie, our younger daughter. We just got back last night*" Elaine responded, "*Oh, that's wonderful. I know it was a long process to make it happen. I know it could take years to adopt a baby.*" Ann responded, letting out a deep breath, "*yes, it seemed like a lifetime, but she is finally here.*"

Elaine went down to her car and Harold followed soon after. A quick, "*congratulations. I'll say hello later. We are running a little late.*" Ann gave a smile and a wave as she sat in the chair next to the playpen. Not a minute went by and Ann jumped up, picked up Sylvie, and said to Marie, "*let's go see if Grandpa Jimmy and Grandma Mary are up.*" They went inside and slowly made their way downstairs to see Ann's parents were awake. Ann's parents had the apartment downstairs. Marie walked over to her Grandpa Jimmy and said, "*see Sylvie.*" He looked up at Ann and Sylvie and a big smile covered his whole face. "*Yes, I see Sylvie. How are you little one?*" Grandpa Jimmy was finishing his eggs as they approached so he quickly cleared his table and moved over his newspaper. Mary was ill and in a wheelchair next to the table. She smiled when she saw Ann and the babies come into their kitchen. Mary said, "*what sweet little bit sunshine she is.*" Ann set Sylvie in her Grandpa Jimmy's arms. His large arms held her safely and he was thrilled he had another granddaughter. Jim asked Ann, "*Did you invite Ella over later?*" Ann responded with, "*next week.*" They have to go somewhere today. Mary could not take her eyes off Sylvie. She knew she was a special baby. After Jim held Sylvie for a few minutes Ann placed Sylvie on Mary's lap. Ann continued to hold Sylvie in place, but Mary was thrilled to have her new granddaughter on her lap. Mary looked up at Ann and said, "*You made my day.*" As Sylvie spent a few minutes on Mary's lap, Jim talked to Marie, only 5 years old. Marie told Jim all about their long car ride, the restaurant they ate in, and the nun they met at the orphanage.

A relaxing first day for Sylvie, Marie, Ann, and Joseph led to a quiet family dinner then a good night's sleep.

Chapter 9

A week later, some family arrived… Sylvie was going to meet Aunt Ella, Uncle Walter, and cousin Diane who was her God Mother. Ella walked in and at first sight of Sylvie said in her bold voice, *"My goodness, she's so skinny. You better fatten her up Ann."* Ann just smiled, walked over to her Aunt Ella and took her coat. It was a nice day with family. Diane handled Sylvie with great care, so gentle.

It was another nice summer day so everyone sat on the porch before dinner. Again neighbors passed as they walked to the corner store and offered well wishes. All the neighbors knew Aunt Ella. She was always the life of the party, offering her honest and often humorous opinion whenever she felt the need. Little Sylvie was passed around and photos were taken. The memories of that day would last a lifetime.

Back inside for dinner, a wide variety of foods to please everyone at the table. Ann always went all-out to please anyone who visited their home. *"Ann, this ham is delicious, how do you do it?"* A quick response from Ann, *"oh, it's nothing. I just put it in the oven."* Conversation went from the good food to what they all though the future would be like. Everyone knew that big sister Marie was highly intelligent so she would have any career she chose, but no one knew anything about little Sylvie yet. The only thing everyone knew was that she needed to gain weight and learn English. "*They spoke to her in French in the orphanage. She only responds to a few words in French.*" Ann commented. Diane responded with, "Don't worry about that. Just speak to her in English and she'll learn. She's young."

Uncle Walter a funny WWII veteran chimed in, "*Have you taken her anywhere yet?*' Of course, Aunt Ella responded with, "*What are you asking that for?*" Joseph and Ann couldn't help but laugh because Uncle Walter and Aunt Ella never seemed to agree on anything. Ann said, "*well, yes, the doctor, the park, and out to the grocery store. She's been pretty good, but gets a little loud when she gets bored.*" Diane, a social worker, reminded Ann it was a good idea to expose Sylvie to as much as possible. "*Eventually Sylvie will get used to being out and about.*" Ann reminded them that before they brought her home she only saw her crib and the inside of that filthy orphanage.

"*How bad could it have been?*" was Aunt Ella's question. Joseph said, "*it was disgusting. I cannot believe they are allowed to operate like that. And the stench could knock you off your feet.*" Everyone agreed that it is good Sylvie left that orphanage when she did. Ann told them the nun said "*Sylvie would end up dying if she stayed there.*" Sylvie really wasn't eating and all she did all day was lie in a crib. The nun said she was getting thinner by the day. "*At a year old what else could she do?*" was Diane's thought. "*It's not like she could control what she did all day. It is actually possible to start to die without food or human interaction.*" Aunt Ella said, "*Oh, really? Are you sure about that Diane?*" Joseph *and* Ann just looked at each other as their relatives disagreed once again.

Over the next several months little Sylvie met the rest of the family, neighbors, and many close friends. The one thing they all said upon first meeting Sylvie was that she was so small for her age. And Ann reminded everyone that she as doing everything she could to help Sylvie gain weight. Ann's usual response was, "*The doctor is not worried. He knows she'll gain weight. I put her back on the bottle and I'm feeding her regular food too.*"

Chapter 10

As time went on Sylvie became very comfortable with her family. She adjusted quite well to seeing people all the time, seeing different surroundings, and being held often. Ann walked around the house holding Sylvie very often. She knew exactly what Sylvie needed, love, a human touch, and good food. And Ann gave her just that. The days were filled with doing normal homemaker activities such as cleaning, cooking, and shopping, but there was something a bit more. When Ann went downstairs to help her parents with their chores Sylvie climbed on her Grandma Mary's wheelchair. Most adults would be horrified at the thought of a toddler climbing on a wheelchair and an ill relative, but Mary absolutely adored Sylvie. She loved that Sylvie was not afraid of the wheelchair and often said to Ann, *"she's going to be an acrobat."* Unfortunately, when Sylvie was just three years old Grandma Mary passed away. Although she was only three when she last saw her Grandma Mary, Sylvie remembered her fondly. She remembered her smile and gentle nature. And she remembered riding on the wheelchair with Grandma Mary.

Sylvie and Grandma Mary both enjoyed being physically close. It almost seemed like a match made in heaven when they were together.

A few years after Grandma Mary's passing, Ann was cleaning out her parent's dressers and closet. Ann with tears in her eyes was throwing out her Mom's old clothes and anything else Grandpa Jimmy no longer needed. She kept asking her father to clean things out, but he could not bring himself to do it and told Ann she could.

Grandpa Jimmy was at work so the apartment was empty and a bit dark. Sylvie was right there with Ann getting into everything that Ann pulled things out of the dresser and closet. Sylvie noticed Ann pulled out a large brown case from the bottom of the closet. Papers were sticking out because it was so over stuffed. Ann started looking at papers in the case and sorted through them. Sylvie, being a curious 6 year old, watched closely to see what was next. It was time for Ann to tell Sylvie that she was adopted. Holding up a few papers in front of Sylvie, "*These are your papers.*" Ann said. Ann knew Sylvie did not really understand. Ann held Sylvie close and said "*you're adopted. We went all the way to Canada to get you.*" Sylvie did not react other than looking at the paper. After a brief glance at the paper, Sylvie felt her mom's hug. It seemed like a special hug ad Ann said, "*I love you.*" to Sylvie. Sylvie could remember the case, the papers coming out of it, and Ann showing her one piece of paper. But more importantly, she remembered that expression on her mom's face and the hug right after she saw the paper. That hug seemed to be all that mattered that day. Sylvie , as young as she was, knew it was a special moment in front of that closet full of old memories.

Sylvie knew it was so special because of the hug and words that followed the papers. She told one of her friends on the block. That parent mentioned it to Ann and Ann was not happy that the other kids knew. But to Sylvie, it meant she was special because her parents went all the way to Canada to pick her up. She felt special because her Mom told her she was special and showed her that with her love every day. Ann did ask Sylvie not to tell everyone because not everyone is adopted or knows how special it is.

At age 6, there was much more talk within her family regarding her adoption. But the fact that Sylvie would soon become an American Citizen was one reason for this conversation. In order to become a citizen one of the things that potential citizens had to do was memorize specific historical facts, state the pledge of allegiance, and give a reason for becoming a citizen. Sylvie was nervous that she would not memorize the facts or meet the other requirements. After all, she was only 6 years old!

The day arrived, Sylvie and Ann entered a large room filled with adults from many different countries. Sylvie watched her mom complete papers and then they waited. Then it was time. Sylvie remained quiet until all potential citizens were asked to repeat after the person leading the ceremony. She repeated every word with her right hand raised and at the end the person leading the long statement said, *"Congratulations, you are now American Citizens*." The room was happy, but not jubilant. It was more of a proud, happy moment than once of loud celebration. All Sylvie knew was that she was happy she did not have to recall the historical events or any of the other requirements the adults were asked to memorize. Ann answered all of the required questions for Sylvie, her picture was taken, and shortly after Sylvie was issued a paper that stated Naturalized Citizen. Not only was Sylvie officially adopted at 14 months of age, she was now an American Citizen. That was it, Sylvie was here to stay!

So throughout childhood, Sylvie displayed Canadian and American flags in her bedroom. Ann and Joseph welcomed her need to remain attached to her French heritage. Sylvie was proud of who she was, French, adopted, and daughter of Ann and Joseph.

For years Sylvie did not mention to anyone outside the family that she was adopted, but .she knew it was special. Grandma Grace told Sylvie about the trip to Canada and their ride back at the border. Sylvie loved that story and began to call herself an "import" like a fine wine. It was a light-hearted humorous type of comment whenever Sylvie called herself an import. Many people laughed at her brief and unique description of her adoption. She knew she had a different start to her life because her family told her the stories of that trip and the efforts it took to bring her home, but she had a normal childhood with Ann and Joseph.

Sylvie's childhood was filled with family dinners, Sunday ice skating, dance classes, summer vacations, winter ski trips, shopping and anything else Ann and Joseph could think of to keep Sylvie and her sister Marie happy and healthy. By the time Sylvie was in school, Ann returned to work. Ann and Joseph were wonderful role models for Sylvie and Marie, hard-working, family first, and they lived an honest life. That was how Sylvie and Marie were raised.

Chapter 11

By the time Sylvie was in high school, she was already working, competing in a sport, and had an active social life. She spent her years in grammar school as a shy young girl, but in high school she seemed to open up and made some nice friends. One day, her new friend Dee mentioned that she was adopted to Sylvie. In amazement, Sylvie's eyes lit up. *"Are you really? Seriously? So am I."* Sylvie could not believe she actually knew someone else who was adopted. Dee then told Sylvie that another girl in their high school was adopted too. Sylvie was shocked that she knew two other people who were adopted. The three girls remained friends during high school and for many years after high school. They must have felt a special understanding that most children could not know. It was not the topic of conversation after a short time, but they seemed to feel that sense of comfort with one another for many years. Their lives brought them in different directions, but the girls were friendly for a long time.

Sylvie always thought being adopted was something special and something to be proud of. She loved life and did not feel any gaps or voids. She had Canadian flags in her bedroom and enjoyed her individuality, but had no reason or desire to find her birth-mom.

Her two friends, Dee and Jan, did search for their birth-mothers and both ended in happy results. Both of them have been in touch with their birth mothers regularly. For them, it was a good decision.

Chapter 12

Sylvie was very close to her dad, Joseph. They did so much together. Both had a love of the water, whether they were in their pool, on Joseph's boat, or at the beach, they were like two peas in a pod. Joseph often showed his forearm to Sylvie to compare his dark tan to Sylvie's light golden tan. Sylvie wanted the same dark tan as her Dad, but that never happened. They enjoyed their time together, especially in the summers. Ann and Sylvie's sister Marie often enjoyed their time together too. Neither of them enjoyed the water or the sun so they went shopping often. Family friends sometimes joked that they each got one child. Every evening they ate dinner together as a family, went on family vacations, and visited relatives as a family. Both Ann and Joseph thought family time was very important.

In 1992, at age 25, Sylvie's dad, Joseph passed away. He had health issues for a long time, but complications from a surgery were the cause of death. Sylvie was heart-broken. She knew it was coming because he was in intensive care for such a long time. The pain of her loss was unbearable. Her dad was her best friend. How would she go on without him? Whenever Sylvie or Marie needed help Joseph was there to save the day. Sylvie recalled to one relative at the funeral, "*when we first moved to Staten Island I got lost on my way home one night. It was very late, after midnight. I was panicked, found a pay phone by a diner, and called home. I told my dad I was lost and he asked me to look up at the street signs and tell home where I was. Dad said he would be right there. He was not even angry. And he showed up in just a few minutes. I was able to follow him home.*" It wasn't far from the new house, but the new house was not easy to find. That was just one example of how Joseph saved the day. And for years to come Joseph had a chuckle whenever that story was told. He knew Sylvie did not like Staten Island, but tried to help her be as happy as possible. There were so many times that Joseph helped his daughters through difficult times. He was truly a family man and taken from them way too soon.

Life was difficult for Sylvie, Marie, and Ann without Joseph. They did adjust to his absence, but it was not easy. Sylvie was hit hard. Ann seemed to change after Joseph passed. And Marie was pretty quiet, mourning in private.

Sylvie only went to the cemetery twice. The second time she collapsed to the ground and wanted to just be in the ground with Joseph. She no longer wanted to live. She sat there crying for hours. Depression was setting in and she did not tell a sole.

Every life stage was difficult without her dad, even many years later. You see, parents and children do not have to be biological parents and children for that unbreakable bond. The people who raise you and love you every day are your parents. Sylvie knew from a young child that she was adopted, but that did not matter. Ann and Joseph have been her parents since the day they took her home.

Chapter 13

Sylvie never had the desire to find her birth-mother, like two of her friends, Dee and Jan, did. She had a full life. But Sylvie did always want to thank her birth-mother for making the right decision of giving her up for adoption. And she did want to know what medical issues ran in her family because that was always a question at doctor appointments.

As an adult, Sylvie was involved in an accident. She suffered multiple injuries and then a year later was diagnosed with fibromyalgia. Sylvie visited many doctors. Other than how she felt that day, the doctors asked about medical history and family history. It was always a bit frustrating to never have an answer to many popular questions. "Does cancer run in your family? Do heart conditions run in your family? And do digestive problems ruin in your family?" Sylvie cringed every time a doctor asked about family history. Her standard response has always been, "*I don't know. I'm adopted.*" Many doctors just moved on, some had a blank expression, and others apologized. Sylvie never understood why any would apologize. Were they apologizing for asking or for her being adopted? She never thought anyone should apologize for either.

Chapter 14

Sylvie ended up going to local colleges and commuting. She did not want to leave her life in Brooklyn. She loved her parents, loved her job, and loved her boyfriend. There was no reason to leave the state or her very full life. In her first college semester, Sylvie was on the Dean's list. That boosted her enthusiasm to continue in her efforts to do well.

At the age of 21 Sylvie bought a business. She kept it running for ten years. Sylvie completed most of her college courses, then running the business became her top priority. She took ten years off from college and focused on building and running her business.

In the tenth year, her business flooded and Sylvie lost everything. She not only lost the income generated, she lost all of the supplies, products, and equipment required to run the business. Her employees were also out jobs. Sylvie felt a great sense of loss, as if mourning the death of a close friend. She did manage to secure jobs for her employees in the same industry and many kept in touch with her for years afterwards.

Chapter 15

Sylvie spent the next year working for another company and applying to law schools. She always knew she wanted to continue her education; she just was not sure what degree she wanted to work towards for a long time. She was on a mission. She completed 40 college credits in another major in just one year in order to get a BA degree. That is what she needed for law school. Sylvie was only 6 credits shy of a BS degree for ten years, but the colleges no longer offered that major when she wanted to complete it. An undergraduate advisor suggested Sylvie completely change her major to get that degree because he had confidence she could get it done within one year.

Sylvie did get the BA Degree and she got an acceptance letter to a small law school. She was also on the waiting list for her favorite law school in NYC. She knew she did not want to wait to get started so she took the spot in the smaller law school out of state.

Sylvie relocated to another state for law school and was off to start a new life. She was excited and ready to do the work for a law degree. Her plan was to work in a prosecutor's office. Things were going as expected. Some classes were very difficult and others required effort, but were tolerable. Sylvie read on average one thousand pages a week in order to keep up with the law school work load. She was doing it. Sylvie was working part time in order to support herself as well. She had no time for a social life, but was thrilled to be studying law.

Chapter 16

Law school was going well, until one day Sylvie got a phone call from an older relative. "*Sylvie, it's cousin Lou. How are you?*" A bit concerned because Sylvie never got phone calls from this cousin Sylvie responded, "*Good. How is everything there? Is everyone OK?*" Lou continued on, "*I got a phone call for you.*" Sylvie getting more concerned and a bit confused, listening carefully. "*Someone said your birth-mother is looking for you. He asked me for your phone number.*" Shocked, Sylvie was at a loss for words at first. Once the shock wore off, Sylvie responded, "*Really? Who was it? How did they get your number?*" Lou explained, "*Not really sure, but they did say they looked up many people with our last names and finally reached me. I did not give them your number.*" Sylvie, a bit disappointed and confused wondered why. "*I took their number for you in case you want to return their call. Is that something you want? Do you want to be in touch with your birth-mother?*" Sylvie thought about it for a moment, "*I always thought about it, but never felt the need to find her. I guess it would be nice to thank her for making the decision she made. And I always wanted to know what diseases run in her family. I don't know if I should call back.*" Lou feeling some compassion responded, "*Think about it before you call. It could change your life. And your mother may get upset. I called her for your number and she seemed a bit upset.*" Now Sylvie was even more confused as to what to do. "*Do I call or not? Now I'm curious, but I hate to upset mom.*" After a little more conversation the call ended. Sylvie just sat quietly on her couch. She was not sure if she should call her mom, call the number, or just pick up on her studying again. She held the number for a few days then decided she wanted to call.

A bit nervous, Sylvie dialed the number in Canada. A man answered. It sounded like a friendly voice so Sylvie identified herself and said she was returning a call. The man on the other end seemed very happy when he heard Sylvie's name. "*Oh, I was hoping you would call. I am a social worker in Canada. I am handling your birth-mother's request to find you. She does not know I found you yet. I want to know if you are interested in receiving letters or meeting her in the future.*"

Sylvie's mind was truly blown. She was not sure how to react. Was she happy or upset? She really did not expect this phone call to ever happen. "*I'm not sure. I did always wonder about her, but never felt the need to search for her. I did always want to thank her for making the right decision though. I had a great childhood.*" The man on the other end, "*That's wonderful. May I tell her I reached you? And do you want to move forward?*" Sylvie without a real answer said, "*I'm not sure.*" The social worker, still with a pleasant voice said, "*Why don't you think about it for a week. I will call you next week and then you can tell me if you want letters or a visit. And if you do not want any part of meeting her you can say that too. I will not tell her I reached you yet. It is up to you whether we move forward and in what capacity.*" Relieved, Sylvie agreed to another call the following week. She hung up the phone, in shock. Out loud she said, "*Oh, my God, what do I do? How could this be happening? It's like a dream, not a great dream, but not a nightmare either.*"

Sylvie could not focus on her school work that night. And she realized she could not focus on her schoolwork any night after that call. She began to struggle with a few classes. Within only one week, Sylvie was falling behind in law school. She figured the initial shock would pass and she would catch up on her school work. She did catch up, but never regained her edge. She continued to struggle in two of her 5 classes.

Chapter 17

In about one week Sylvie received another phone call from the social worker in Canada. *"How are you doing today? I still did not tell your birth-mother I found you."* Sylvie was relieved to hear that, *"Thanks so much. I appreciate that."* He then asked, *"Did you think about what you want to do? I will do whatever it is you want. You can have her write a letter, meet her, or never let her know you were found."* It was so much for Sylvie to think about. She knew some people would have loved to meet their birth-mother while others would have slammed the phone down. Sylvie was not like either of those. She knew she had no desire to meet her birth-mother now. *"I am still not sure. I'm in law school now and can't come to Canada. I'm not really sure I ever want to meet her, but I would like her to thank her for the decision she made. I imagine it was not easy."* The social worker, *"You're right. She struggled with her decision all her life. She looked for you for many years without success before she came to me. My job is to make sure neither of you gets hurt. It is really up to you how we proceed."* Sylvie gave it some thought and then asked, *"What if she just sent a letter? Would she have my address then?"* He reassured Sylvie, *"Oh, no. She would give the letter to me in a sealed envelope. I would then put it in anther envelope to send it to you. I would not read it, unless you want me to screen it."*

Feeling a little better about the situation, Sylvie agreed to receive a letter. She figured it couldn't hurt. She told the social worker a little about her life, that she had a wonderful childhood, filled with loving relatives, active days, vacations, and good schools, and she has a sister, but always wanted a brother. He was very happy a good family adopted me and ended the call after taking her address and wishing her well.

The anticipation of waiting for that letter was exciting. Day and night Sylvie wondered what would be written in it. Would there be photos? Does she have any siblings? What has her birth-mother done with her life since? And with all the excitement, Sylvie could not focus on her law school work. She tried, but could not seem to stay focused. It seemed very few minutes her mind wandered to what her birth-mother would write in a letter or what she would look like. Sylvie hoped she would get a picture in the letter.

Chapter 18

"*Oh, my God, it's here. I can't believe they sent it so quickly*!" were Sylvie's thoughts as she took her mail out of her mailbox. She was so excited that she talked to her self loudly. A look from a neighbor she nearly bumped into made Sylvie realize she was speaking out loud as she hurried away from the mail box.

Sylvie quickly ran up the stairs and into her apartment. She dropped her bag and took one long look at the envelope before she carefully opened it. She did not want to tear through the return address or any of the writing. She then slowly opened the inside envelope and a few pictures dropped out. "*She sent pictures*!" Sylvie felt the goose bumps all over as she picked up the picture off the floor and turned it over. Talking to herself, Sylvie said, "*Holy cow, I look like her. Oh, wow, I have two brothers! I can't believe this. I always wanted a brother.*"

Still in shock Sylvie proceeded to unfold the letter. It was handwritten and the paper seemed to be very old and fragile, maybe even handmade paper from a craft store. Sylvie sat on the couch to begin reading.

"Hello Sylvie… a little letter to describe myself… My name is Denise…What made me want to meet you is that someone close to me went through that experience and it was really beautiful and positive experience… It shook me and I went into therapy…"

Sylvie could not believe what she was reading because only a few years before that two of her friends searched out their birth mothers and had good experiences. It seems Sylvie and her birth-mother both saw people they knew reunited after many years. Both saw the happiness it brought their friends. But the difference is that Sylvie never had the NEED to search for her birth-mother. She was curious, but did not feel that void in her life.

Sylvie read more of the letter and it opened her eyes. Her birth-mother now had a name, a personality, and she was a REAL person. How was this possible after a lifetime of not thinking of her as a regular person? Sylvie had questions throughout life, but never NEEDED the answers. She asked older relatives as a child who she looked like. That is one thing that she always wanted to know. Sylvie knew growing up she did not look like her parents or big sister. It was a curiosity, but not a bothersome issue.

Now, all of a sudden she had some answers and photos. She finally knew who she looked like. This led to more questions and now the NEED for some more answers. This letter piqued Sylvie's interest, but she knew she did not want to actually meet her birth-mother, at least not yet.

The letter included… "*I'm divorced, but from that marriage have two sons, your brothers.*" Sylvie felt goose bumps all over when she read about her brothers. She always wanted a brother. The older of the two is seven years younger than Sylvie and the other is eleven years younger than her. Sylvie now had the brother she always wanted, times two. But how would she ever meet them or even speak with them?

More of the letter revealed that Sylvie's birth-mother went country dancing once a week, took care of a dog and a cat, had arthritis, and took care of elderly people. Wow, some of the same things Sylvie has done. Was it nature or nurture in this case? How could it be that Sylvie and her birth-mother both spent time each week dancing, loved animals, and suffered from arthritis? Both have had jobs caring for sick and elderly people too. Sylvie studied physical therapy and in later years was an Emergency

Medical Technician. In an odd way, Sylvie followed in some of her birth-mother's (Denise's) footsteps. But how could that be?

Sylvie read the letter several times. It arrived just before Thanksgiving. She brought it home when she went to celebrate Thanksgiving with her family. Sylvie had a great relationship with her family. It hurt her to see her mom, Ann, so upset that she was found by her birth-mother. Ann shed some tears when she saw the letter and photos. Sylvie's older cousin Dee was very calm and practical. She was trying to keep Ann from becoming more upset. Dee reminded everyone that with computers and private investigators this was the new reality, whether they liked it or not. She pointed out that Sylvie resembled her birth-mother. And she thought it was interesting to see her sons in one photo. Ann, trying to hold back tears said, "*I'm the one who raised you. I am your mother and will always be your mother. I taught you how to speak, changed your diapers, and have been here every day since we brought you home.*" Sylvie felt terrible that her mom was so upset and responded with, "*Of course I know that. I didn't ask to meet her. She found me.*" Other family members passed around the photos and letter. They wondered why she chose now to find Sylvie until they read the letter saying she saw someone else reunited. Sylvie's big sister was pretty quiet during all of this conversation. She too was adopted, but years before and from the NYC adoption agency. Sylvie wondered if her big sister was also upset with this situation. Turmoil would be the one word to describe Sylvie's emotions this weekend.

Sylvie felt a great deal of excitement and shock after getting this letter. And then she saw the reaction of her family, each one taking turns looking at the letter and photos. Sylvie was truly torn between two worlds.

She knew she did not have to choose between her mom, Ann, and her birthmother, but she did feel like Ann wanted Sylvie to stop the communication with her birth-mother. Ann was hurting. She RAISED Sylvie. How dare her birth-mother intrude and ask to meet her.

Ann told Sylvie when she was young that it was a closed adoption. That meant that neither party could contact the other. The fact that this happened was truly a shock to Ann and the rest of the family. Ann could not hide the pain in her face the entire weekend after seeing that letter from Sylvie's birth-mother.

Chapter 19

It was exciting, exhausting, and really traumatic to be found by her birth-mother. Sylvie did not know what to do. She returned home after her long Thanksgiving weekend and had to catch up on schoolwork. She was a law student and not studying enough ever since this contact was initially made.

From the first phone call Sylvie had trouble focusing on anything else. All she could think about was what her birth-mother could be like. What was her personality like? What has she done all of these years? Did she remember her birthday each year? What was she doing right now? And was her life now in turmoil too?

Sylvie wondered if she knew the impact her birth-mother had on her ever since the first contact. Did she know that she totally disrupted her life?

Sylvie wrote back. She asked what diseases ran in the family and what her nationality was. Sylvie's parents were told that she is 100% French, but Sylvie wanted that confirmed. Sylvie said thank you in the letter too. She always wanted to thank her birth-mother for making the right decision because she had such a good life.

Two weeks later another letter arrived. Sylvie got some more answers, but not what she expected. She learned that stomach issues ran in the family and there were twins in the family. She also learned that no major health issues such as heart disease or cancer ran in the family. Those were the easy answers. Then when it came time to read the ONE question Sylvie wanted answered most there was a change in tone. Sylvie desperately wanted to know her nationality. Was she really 100% French?

In the letter, "*I am very impressed with your life, you seem very determined and talented… All that helps me to accept the decision I made at your birth…I could not have given you security, stability, and the love of a family at the time*"

In the letter, her birth-mother, Denise, went on to discuss her sad childhood with a lot of fear, abuse, and without love. She was helpless and overwhelmed by what was happening. She then went on to tell Sylvie that she "*was raised in fear and violence, abuses of all types.*" Her own mother left her and four siblings when she was young. She wrote, "*my oldest sister ended up in an institution for girls who suffered incest.*" Sylvie's birth-mother, Denise, did not know that until years later. She was then the oldest female of the siblings.

Luckily for Denise, her father was not home all the time. But when he did come home, he brought friends with him. These friends and her father abused Denise on multiple occasions. Her letter included, "*I cannot say more, but at 18 I became pregnant with you… It is still very hard for me to talk about my painful past in spite of all of the therapy.*"

This letter is what crushed Sylvie. She started to feel light-headed as she finished reading the long, difficult letter. Sylvie was now at her breaking point. She asked herself, "*Was it true? Am I really the result of incest and rape?*" How could Sylvie deal with this? Why did her birth-mother, Denise tell her this in a letter? She wrote, "*It is our past that is difficult. One would like to forget, but nothing is forgettable.*"

After the shocking news, the closing of the letter was kind and thoughtful. After several pages discussing the abuse she endured and how Sylvie was conceived. "*Rest assured. I do not want to take anything away from your family. I am simply so grateful. And I will respect all your future decisions. Your family gave you everything I could not."*

Despite the nice ending of the letter, Sylvie spent days and nights crying for months. Was she crying for the pain her birthmother endured or because she found out that she was the result of incest or abuse? Was that why her birth-mother gave her up? It was not just a fun night between two teenagers as the orphanage stated. It was a horrible story of ongoing family abuse for many years.

Sylvie did not know what to do with this information and never wrote another letter.

Chapter 20

With the depression, Sylvie fell deeper and deeper behind in her studies. She struggled to focus on her reading and exams. Sylvie promised herself she would regain focus. But each time she thought she could regain focus there was another thought about her birth-mother or a distraction. Sylvie was trying to start a new life in law school and it was being totally torn apart by of the poor timing of her birth-mother, Denise.

Sylvie stopped all communication with Denise and the social worker. She just could not respond to any more letters or phone calls. Sylvie realized she could not live in confusion or deal with the distraction anymore. She HAD to put this behind her and try to pass her final exams in law school.

Sylvie was going through so much all at once. Being away from her family for law school, dealing with this turmoil alone, and then trying to pass law school and work enough to pay her rent made for a very difficult life. Something HAD to go and it was the craziness of being found by her birth-mother.

On the phone with one of her friends Sylvie said, "*I wasn't even SUPPOSED to be found. How could this happen?*" Being there for Sylvie through everything, her best friend just replied with "*I really don't know. But no one says you HAVE to keep writing or answering their phone calls. You can tell them you need to concentrate on school and can't deal with this distraction now. Maybe when you're done with law school you can pick it up.*" Sylvie liked the refreshing and sensible advice from her friend. "*I did just decide to stop communicating. I should have asked your opinion months ago. I might not have received that last letter if I did. Thanks!*"

The call ended with Sylvie and her best friend. Sylvie felt a little surge of energy for the first time since October. It was now April, about six months after the start of this insane disruption of her life.

Sylvie now had a plan. Study like crazy for her final exams, hope she would pass every one of them, and then start the next semester with a clear mind. Next semester she would not only pass every exam, she would do well.

Final exams did not go so well for Sylvie. She got the second highest grade on one exam, was in the middle of the class on two other exams, and failed one exam miserably. That one failure caused her to be dismissed from law school for a low GPA. It was only low by a few points, but the school did not want to make an exception or allow her to repeat that class. Sylvie's dream of becoming a lawyer had come to an end, thanks in part to the poor timing and shocking news from her birth-mother.

What was she going to do now? There were no other goals in mind for Sylvie. Sylvie's plan was to be in law school for four years, graduate, and then get a job in a law firm. She had a nice life planned that was totally derailed. Now what?

Chapter 21

Sylvie met a nice guy during this life of chaos at her job. It was nothing serious because she was trying to focus on staying afloat in law school. She only occasionally dated him. He did not have much of an opinion as far as her birth-mother was concerned and he likely had no idea just how much it bothered her.

Now there was no more law school. Sylvie needed to find a good job and rethink her future. There was more time for dating and searching to find out if she could apply to other law schools. She submitted a formal letter to ask if she could remain in the law school and repeat the class, but was not allowed to do that. The fact that she was dismissed because her GPA went just below the acceptable level she could not apply to any other law schools for two years. Her life was in shambles.

Sylvie found a good job a few months later. She enjoyed her work, spent more time going out with her boyfriend, and took more trips home to see her family. Things were sort of back to normal, but would never be the same.

If anything good came of this attempted reunion, it was that Sylvie became closer to her mom, Ann. After the initial shock wore off and life returned to normal, conversations between them became more relaxed and natural again.

Life went on for Sylvie and her family.

Chapter 22

In the following years after she left law school, Sylvie ended up getting married, starting a business with her husband, suffering spinal damage from an accident, and moving closer to her family. Her life ended up being very different from her original goals and plans, but Sylvie has been satisfied with an interesting life. One friend recently said to Sylvie, "*You've certainly done a lot of living.*"

Sylvie still has much more life to live with some career goals to reach. She never had children of her own and has been divorced.

With her 50th birthday and her upcoming 50th anniversary of being adopted, Sylvie wanted to revisit the idea of reuniting with her birth-mother. After all, she is not in law school and has a more simple life now. The distraction would not ruin her career goals or family life.

Sylvie kept the letters the entire time, nearly twenty years after she received them. It took almost twenty years for Sylvie to open the letters again. This time with more life experience and less emotion she read through the letters. There was still a little sting, knowing how she was conceived, but she has come to terms with it. At this point, it did not matter how she came into the world, only that she will leave it a better place before she dies.

Now it was time to tell her story. She was now strong enough to bring back the memories. No depression or sadness, just a desire to share.

Sylvie wanted to reach her brothers more than her birth-mother. She did always want a brother and why not get to know the two she had? She reached out to the social worker who did remember the case all these years later. His response in an email was, "*I am no longer in contact with her, but try reaching out through the organization.*" He gave the name of the organization and the city where they were located.

Sylvie has had this information for a while now and is trying to decide whether she really should open this can of worms or leave it alone. Sylvie could not believe she actually reached the social worker and he sent such a fast response.

Was Sylvie feeling that void now, all these years later that adopted children say they feel? How could that be? She has had such a good childhood, an amazing family, everything she ever needed, and she still has a good relationship with her mom, Ann. What made her reach out in her 50th year here?

Maybe when you reach 50 years old, you realize your life is more than half over. It's time to do things you want to do before you get too old or die. Sylvie is not sure what type of response she would get from her brothers if they are reached. In one of the letters, Denise, her birth-mother stated her brothers wanted to know more about her. Would it be a good time? Would their lives be disrupted or would they welcome the distraction?

Sylvie was hesitant because she did not want to hurt them if the disruption was not welcome at this point, but how would she know unless she tried. Her birth-mother is approaching 70. At that age would she want to be bothered? After all, she was the one to look for Sylvie.

There are so many unanswered questions with adoptions. Can they ever all be answered?

Sylvie suggests, if you are part of an adoption, either the child or the birth-mother, give it thought before you reach out to find someone. Sometimes there are things going on in their lives that cannot be interrupted, such as law school for Sylvie. Her birth-mother finding her changed the entire direction of her life. Be sure you take that into consideration before you make the call. Being found IS very traumatic and it wears on your heart. It is difficult to deal with even if both people want to reunite and start a relationship of some sort. Being reunited can be a beautiful thing, but it can also cause terrible problems with the families. Being found can even break up otherwise happy families.

Sylvie's friend's mom gave up a baby when she was young and no one in the family knew. When that baby turned 50 she found her birth-mother and caused many problems with their family. Sylvie's friend's mom did not want to be found, was upset when she was found, and turned her birth-child away.

Chapter 23

Many adoptions end up in happy lives for all involved. The decision could not be easy to give up a child, but it is the right one most of the time. The child often ends up in a great home and has a happy life. Closed adoptions should continue, but with the internet, private investigators, and tech savvy people, it is possible to find people who do not want to be found. It is a different world now than it was in 1967 when Sylvie was officially adopted. Closed adoptions are no longer a guarantee of privacy.

Sylvie's one piece of advice to any family interested in adopting a child is to tell them when they are young. Remind them it is a great thing and that you worked hard to bring them home. And most importantly, remind them daily that you are their family. The people who raise a child are that child's parents. And be sure to give them that full life so that they do not feel a void or need to search for another family. If a child is satisfied that all their needs are being met they might not feel a NEED to search.

This was based on Sylvie's story, her adoption. A few conversations may not be exact quotes. They are from stories told to Sylvie by family throughout her life and memories of events and conversations. All of the names have been changed to protect the privacy of Sylvie's family and friends. Sylvie is her original name, but her name was changed upon adoption.

If there is ever contact again, there will be a second edition of this book to include the outcome.

You may reach Sylvie through email at **TheSylvieGStory@gmail.com.**

Made in United States
North Haven, CT
08 January 2022